Once Upon A Dream

The Book Of Words

Edited By Lynsey Evans

First published in Great Britain in 2024 by:

YoungWriters
Est. 1991

Young Writers
Remus House
Coltsfoot Drive
Peterborough
PE2 9BF
Telephone: 01733 890066
Website: www.youngwriters.co.uk

All Rights Reserved
Book Design by Ashley Janson
© Copyright Contributors 2024
Softback ISBN 978-1-83565-859-8
Printed and bound in the UK by BookPrintingUK
Website: www.bookprintinguk.com
YB0608A

FOREWORD

Welcome Reader, to a world of dreams.

For Young Writers' latest competition, we asked our writers to dig deep into their imagination and create a poem that paints a picture of what they dream of, whether it's a make-believe world full of wonder or their aspirations for the future.

The result is this collection of fantastic poetic verse that covers a whole host of different topics. Let your mind fly away with the fairies to explore the sweet joy of candy lands, join in with a game of fantasy football, or you may even catch a glimpse of a unicorn or another mythical creature. Beware though, because even dreamland has dark corners, so you may turn a page and walk into a nightmare!

Whereas the majority of our writers chose to stick to a free verse style, others gave themselves the challenge of other techniques such as acrostics and rhyming couplets. We also gave the writers the option to compose their ideas in a story, so watch out for those narrative pieces too!

Each piece in this collection shows the writers' dedication and imagination – we truly believe that seeing their work in print gives them a well-deserved boost of pride, and inspires them to keep writing, so we hope to see more of their work in the future!

CONTENTS

Independent Entrants

Dylan Potter (11)   1

Audley Junior School, Blackburn

Zakariya Butt (11)   2
Zara Mulla (11)   4
Umaymah Mulla (11)   5
Maryam Bashir (11)   6
Aaminah Mulla (10)   7
Abdullah Khan (11)   8

Bandon Hill Primary School, Wallington

Nikhil Aubeelauck (10)   9
Sofia Johnson-Boateng (10)   10
Jenanthan Eswaran (11)   12
Aurora Anstey (10)   14
Rithika Raveenthiran (11)   15
Devanshi Anoop (10)   16
Ileana Aubeelauck (9)   17
Salih Mohamed Liyas (11)   18
Aarav Hungsraz (9)   19
Jayden Oguntoyinbo (9)   20
Mithran Muralendran (11)   21
Phoenix Williams (8)   22
Jack Spencer (11)   23
Sophie Oguntoyinbo (11)   24
Kexin Luo (10)   25
Romeesa Khan (9)   26
Florence Macdonald (11)   27
Rhys Phillips (10)   28
Anay Nair (10)   29
Aakash Gandavadi (10)   30

Jahmya-Jade Monica Powell (10)   32
Aaron Bijoy (10)   33
Vivaan Mahesh (11)   34
Sebastian Dixon (11)   35
Nashai Kerr (11)   36
Disha Sudhakaran (10)   37
Maximus Seear (11)   38
Sheydaen Lahilthan (10)   40
Sebastian Rankin (9)   41
Anay Chaturvedi (10)   42
Gloria Denovagyte-Valantinaite (9)   43
Abishali Ravinthiran (8)   44
Dami Adeyemo (9)   45
Samanvi Nagasri Vadlamudi (11)   46
Emilia Tett (11)   47
Ella Sorel (10)   48
Nikhil Nibu Kuriakose (11)   49
Isla Lacey (10)   50
Zeynab Kafizas (10)   51
Reshmi Ramamoorthi (10)   52
Blake Turner (10)   53
Zainab Munawar (9)   54
Shirley Guo (7)   55
Kerem Colak (10)   56
Milo Cheng (10)   57
Elsie Noble (11)   58
Penny Polley (11)   59
Lara Suvari (10)   60
Sonny Mistry (10)   61
Pragya Bhadani (11)   62
Mawuena Badasu (7)   63
Evelyn Nkrumah (9)   64
Isla Summerfield (7)   65
Aahan Nath (10)   66
Shri Sankalp Maryala (11)   67

Piero Jara Ortega (7)	68
Josh Hyland (9)	69
Charlie Nicol (11)	70
Saraneya Arulmugan (9)	71
Tanatswa Taruvamba (9)	72
Libby Roberts (9)	73
Umar Najimudeen (9)	74
Ali Khan (10)	75
Tori Trinidad (10)	76
Sidney Devereux-Gent (9)	77
Thomas Banks (10)	78
Jeremy Qin (8)	79
Aria Cleghorn (7)	80
Krishnujan Kannathasan (9)	81
Miya Cheng (8)	82
Jaiwin Kalaicheivan (7)	83
Jasper Liem (11)	84
Esin Vaid (7)	85
Bentley Good (7)	86
Milan Patel (9)	87
Samantha Adielle Magesh (10)	88
Isha Nayak (7)	89
Mithulan Pirabaharan (8)	90
Yago Bañuelos (9)	91
Livvy Griscti (7)	92
Nathanael Mullings	93
Tilly Turner (10)	94
Filip Grabowski (7)	95
Lucas Mackin (7)	96
Poppy Baldwin (10)	97
Katie Duke (7)	98
Kristian Wilkins (9)	99
Oscar Saunders (10)	100

Cippenham Primary School, Slough

Mollie Baca Jackson (9)	101
Julia Wenderlich (10)	102
Arsh Pannu (10)	104
Michael Amery	106
Aariya Mistry (9)	107
Musa Talib (10)	108
Sunny Singh Johal (10)	109

Alfie Webb (10)	110
Benyamin Fiotmane (10)	112
Ibrahim Butt (9)	113
Zoha Ihsan (9)	114
Maya Deliu (10)	115
Saimaathmika Prasad (10)	116
Kushank Saini (10)	117
Arsal Nasir (10)	118
Rahma Bouzid (10)	119
Noah Heath	120

Glebe Primary School, Kenton

Sofia Jivani (8)	121
Jayan Hirani (8)	122
Aarish Morani (8)	123
Mahi Shah (8)	124
Elisabeth Toma (8)	125
Kiyana Patel (8)	126
Aaditya Rathod (7)	127
Aahana Sahai (7)	128
Tiana Rabadia (8)	129
Krisha Jayswal (8)	130

Gunter Primary School, Pype Hayes

Eevee Brookes (8)	131
Romé Hamilton (8)	132
Aidan Ly (9)	134
Arabella Swan Jones (8)	136
Kian Lo (9)	138
Chloe Hodgetts (8)	140
Ollie Davis (8)	141
Isha Adams (9)	142
Aadham Daud (8)	143
TJ Cox (8)	144
Rhema Theophilus Okere (9)	145
Hannah Khan (7)	146
Juliet Jenkinson (9)	147
Chloe Evans (9)	148
Erin Clarke (9)	149
Savannah Grant (8)	150
Aurora Maxfield-Foster (9)	151

I'miah-Milan Jackson Griffiths (8)	152
Cheyenne Davies (8)	153
Aleeza Minhas (9)	154
Amelia Reynolds (8)	155
Sebastian Ullah (9)	156
Bobby Thomas (9)	157
Zayn Shaikh (8)	158
Lucas Ma (8)	159
Aisha Adetona (8)	160
Kalelsi Macalum Francis (8)	161
Zac Moore (8)	162
Kirsten Dhliwayo (9)	163
Ibrahim Hedjem (8)	164
Aria-Rae Delaney (7)	165
Freya Jordan (8)	166
Weronika Aiken (8)	167
Michael Waltham (9)	168
Rhyleigh-Marie Thompson (9)	169

THE CREATIVE WRITING

Me

In the future I dream my goals,
And also, I build on other goals,
I hope to be myself,
And not to distract anybody else,
I wish to be able to be me,
And be able to be free.

Dylan Potter (11)

A Dark Light

I glance to my left and tremble to my right
A blood-curdling howl pierces the nebulous night
Here I stand, far from home,
"But where is here?" rumbles a menacing tone
There you stand, rooted to the ground
Not long left till you'll be found!

Far, far in the darkening distance
A glow begins to swell
My heart raises its hand in hope
Perhaps all will be well
Rising smoke begins to part
And I suddenly notice the beat of a far more wicked heart

I focus on the light and with growing horror I see...
Not a way out, but monstrous fangs gleaming murderously at me

As the flames scurry forth their talons
In this unforeseen suffocating Hell
Somewhere from within my petrified lungs
A guttural voice begins to yell

"You must break free
Of the very fear that has you chained
Only if you believe
Shall the beast be slain!"

I glance to my left and tremble to my right
Is it possible for this nightmare to be survived?
Is this conviction just a dream?
Or a promise I'll be alright?

I glance to my left and tremble to my right
And with a rebellious cry and all my might
I leap into the heart of my fear,
My body jolts up
And my vision becomes clear

I am in bed
On a quiet, peaceful night
And as the thundering hooves of my heart become steady
It whispers
"Everything is alright."

Zakariya Butt (11)
Audley Junior School, Blackburn

Footballer's Dream

In her dreams every night,
Footballers dribble and turn her life from dark to light,
Suddenly, he appears in front of her,
And then, she can see the treasure,
The one she imagined, the one she wanted to meet,
Down her back, could feel the heat,
At the stadium she loves, at the stadium she adores,
She only asked for one more,
To share a pitch with him,
But the chances were very slim,
It happened, she did it, she fulfilled her dream,
Appeared, appeared the team,
She jumped in the air, being full of joy as she played on the pitch,
But then, all of a sudden, there was a switch,
Now it was obvious, it was all just a dream,
A dream she wished was her reality...

Zara Mulla (11)
Audley Junior School, Blackburn

Immortal Being

I 'm stuck in a loop, can't find a way out,
M aybe I can find help if I scream and shout,
M y home planet has been destroyed,
O nly myself and I are left in this void,
R ats lay strewn everywhere and so do the corpses,
T he same fate for the dogs and horses,
A ll of this seems like a dream,
L ike looking at the stars whilst canoeing in the stream,

B ut everything is real,
E very dinner is just a silent meal,
I am trapped in this labyrinth,
N obody can tell me that this is a myth,
G ood thing I still have my sanity...

Umaymah Mulla (11)
Audley Junior School, Blackburn

The Dream Ice Can See

I n my dreams, I can see,
C inderella in her sparkly dress,
E asily reaching out to the sea,

S o much to confess.
K new the girl of his dreams,
A h, but for him I'm a bunch of screams,
T here was another beam of Cupid,
I n his heart, it runs over me, as if I'm stupid.
N ow I'm here, ice skating,
G reetings with flickering fingers of ice

As she leaves the room with my goal

"Oh, ice skating aren't you free?"
"Oh, ice skating am I to be?"

Maryam Bashir (11)
Audley Junior School, Blackburn

Harry Potter

H arry Potter, the boy who lived
A ngry with Voldemort for what he did
R on and Hermoine, Harry's best friends
R eally, a ghost whose neck bends
Y owch! Harry's wiggly arm

P otions going through Harry's palm
O ut they go for Quidditch
T ricks done by Snape's wrists
T reks to find a man from Azkaban who needs pills
E vidence Death Eaters want to kill
R unning through the Forbidden Forest instead of being still.

Aaminah Mulla (10)
Audley Junior School, Blackburn

Candyland Dreamer

Crumbs of ginger behind a candy cane
Twizzler chains and marshmallows below
The yellow cello beneath the tasty jello
Lollipops and gummy treetops
Chocolate bars and chocolate bricks
All around white, dairy and milk
Gummy sharks full of blended sweets
The only thing that is not such a delight to eat

Tempted to bite into the dented chocolate stick
As I go to take a munch
I wake up with a surprise of fruit punch
If only my bed was made out of
Chocolate-flavoured gingerbread...

Abdullah Khan (11)
Audley Junior School, Blackburn

My Homework Ate The Dog!

Last night I had a dream, in which my homework ate my dog.
It was a day when there was just fog,
Until my homework ate my dog.

I went to school with a smirk on my face,
I remember scrunched-up paper all over the place!
My classmates were having a paper aeroplane race
Or maybe, they were all just shouting at Grace!

When school started all we did was work
Until there was a huge berserk!
Then school ended, and we all received our homework.

At home, I was sitting on a log
But then my homework went to eat my sock!
I chased it all the way to the bog
But then it went for my dog!

My little doggy got very soggy
My palms were unbelievably sweaty
Luckily, it was just a dream
When I realised, my face lit up like a beam
But then, hang on, my dog was nowhere to be seen!

Nikhil Aubeelauck (10)
Bandon Hill Primary School, Wallington

Dream About Your Future

I can be a footballer or a baker, maybe even a gymnast.
I have a dream!
What will it be?

F ootball I will play,
O pen goal, everyone will say *hooray!*
O pinions will be made,
T eammates and I will never be afraid!
B alls will be kicked,
A lways be ready,
L earn from my mistakes,
L eap into the crowd!

B aking is my hobby,
A lways try something new!
K icking cakes will always be fun,
E verything will be different,
R ed velvet is my favourite!

G reat scores I will get!
Y ou and the crowd will scream my name,
M y flips will blow you away!
N o one can stop me!

A re you blown away?
S ome people may doubt,
T hat is okay, but I will do it my way.

I can be a footballer or a baker, maybe even a gymnast.
I have a dream!
What will it be?

Sofia Johnson-Boateng (10)
Bandon Hill Primary School, Wallington

Three Worlds, One Boy

Being unloved and weak,
Then rising to your dreams,
You embody a beast,
Anything is your feast,
You're on a roll,
Then there is a sudden fall.

A little boy,
Has so much joy,
He eats a fruit,
Then he becomes a rubber brute,
He tries to be the pirate king,
Willing to fight anything,
He becomes a god,
Breaks his strength pod,
Pirates ready to fight in a long queue,
Now it is to be continued.

The Battle of Gods,
The last rod,
God of Thunder for the Greeks,
The best commander for the weak,
The father of all sons,
The God of all Gods start to run,

The God of the sea,
And the samurai of glee,
The weak won,
So now it's two one.

Going from world to world,
In a magic water whirl,
I see joy,
From the little boy.

Jenanthan Eswaran (11)
Bandon Hill Primary School, Wallington

I Have A Dream

I have a dream to be a performer to dance the night away
I have a dream to be a perfect football player to score loads of goals
I have a dream to be a baker to bake for the Royal Family
I have a dream to be a teacher to teach the best class
I have a dream to be a dance teacher to teach amazing skills
I have a dream to be a hairdresser to braid and wash all types of people's hair
I have a dream to be a YouTuber to reach one million views
I have a dream to be a doctor to care for loads of people
I have a dream to be a vet to look after animals
I have a dream to be a mechanic to fix loads of cars
I have a dream to be an author to write amazing stories
I have a dream to be a firefighter to put out even the biggest fires
I have a dream to be a police officer to put bad guys in jail.
What's your dream?

Aurora Anstey (10)
Bandon Hill Primary School, Wallington

The Chocolate Nightmare

I thought I would wake up in bed,
But I woke up in the darkest dread,
It was the moment of a never-ending dream,
This dream was tasty, sweet but mean.

It started when me and my friend got picked up by a lorry,
My friends said they were sorry...
As we got off, we reached a school,
We entered with no rule.

To find out it was a chocolate factory,
We looked up to see the boss grinning, satisfactory,
He gave us the instructions,
To make our chocolate, we need gumption.

But to end this nightmare, we needed to end the boss,
His name was Ross,
We needed to push him down,
He was above the chocolate spinner,
One, two, three and down he went.

I woke up to see a chocolate bar beside me,
I bit it, but then...
Spiders crawled out my mouth.

Rithika Raveenthiran (11)
Bandon Hill Primary School, Wallington

In My Sleep

When the lights go off and I get under the blanket,
As soon as I close my eyes, the light of dreams goes on.
Testing my knowledge on difficult riddles while a kaleidoscope of my favourite flavours tickles my tastebuds.
Rare flowers growing around me and joy in everyone,
No harmful tricks or pranks anywhere the eye can see.
Children smiling, creativity flowing, just in a world of wonder,
When books fly with mystery and magic and an endless supply of snacks.
There is one danger lurking in the distance,
The door to nightmares.

Where shrieks and screams of fear and pain are heard,
And zombies look for brains.
Everything is dark with blood on streets,
Murders and they're on the loose.
Frowns and tears on every face,
The only thing that would wake me up in my sleep.

Devanshi Anoop (10)
Bandon Hill Primary School, Wallington

Unexpectedly

U p in the sky, here comes a dream
N ow Elen, Nina and Tina read a book to the class
E len touches a bright purple mark and *boom!*
X *xxzzxx...* This is the noise when the three girls suddenly appear in the book.
P andora, the red, scary monster, lives in that village and they are right where she lives!
"E len!" squeals Tina, but too late, Pandora has already grabbed her
"C ome up with a plan quick, Tina," screams Nina
T ina's mind has gone completely blank though
E len suddenly comes back, so there is no point in a plan
D elighted, they are now back in the classroom
L ittle do they know though
Y usuf, another boy, has now gone missing...

Ileana Aubeelauck (9)
Bandon Hill Primary School, Wallington

The Ride On The Rocket

I once had a dream,
I was with a team,
With a band of all my good friends,
We couldn't mask or pretend,
How joyous we were,
As we soared through the sky,

I noticed the stars,
Which were always ever so far,
I felt a longing in my heart,
As I watched these glimmering diamonds,
Pass by my eyes.

I saw Mercury then Earth, Venus and Mars,
We raced by Jupiter, by its many moons and stars,
We passed by Saturn, its rings so big and bright,
Then we saw Uranus and Neptune, as cold and dark as night
As we zoomed through the sky.

We laughed and had fun,
And our enjoyment weighed a tonne,
It was too good to be true,
As we soared through the starry night sky.

Salih Mohamed Liyas (11)
Bandon Hill Primary School, Wallington

Space Search

I am not prepared for this endless darkness
How Mars erupts in my ears
The volcanoes roar to their boundaries
My body cackles
The stars are like stepping stones in a lake
I travel to Jupiter to see a creature
Surprised, I see one
The sun is under me as I drop into the ring of Saturn
Dust turning to aliens
I say, "Hello."
They wave at me and then send me to the Planet of Ice, Uranus
I turn into an ice monster
What a surprise
I travel to Neptune
Ice and wind are like Zeptune
Pluto is an abandoned planet
I travel in the Tardis
The galaxies are like music in my ears
The stars explode into a masterpiece
I finally travel to the end of space.

Aarav Hungsraz (9)
Bandon Hill Primary School, Wallington

A Wild Imagination

Once upon a dream, my imagination ran free,
It was busy, busy as a bee,
It climbed up a tree, it swam in the sea,
But before I continue, what will your imagination be?

It saw a dream of a star,
Even one with a million chocolate bars!
Another with flying cars,
And very surprising dancing jars!

Talking cows were jumping around the place,
Chickens were farting at my face,
Cheetahs were running a million times the pace,
Soon, I saw hippos in space!

My imagination came into my head with a little creep,
Just to make sure I opened my eyes with a little peep,
I was very happy to see it go to sleep,
But before I knew it, I was fast asleep!

Jayden Oguntoyinbo (9)
Bandon Hill Primary School, Wallington

The Day Everything Changed

I imagined a day when everything changed,
Where the good became the bad,
Where the intellectuals became the fools,
Where the rich became poor beggars,
Where a random eleven year old like me became famous!

Where the tooth fairy became a reality,
Where your friend became your worst enemy,
Where less was more and more was less,
Where nightmares became dreams,
Where the monster under the bed made an exit,
Where the Earth was actually flat!

Welcome to the dream I had two years ago, my friend!
As you can see, I was crazy when I was a nine year old,
If you were as well,
That's amazing, because you see,
You would have unique dreams like me!

Mithran Muralendran (11)
Bandon Hill Primary School, Wallington

Nightmare With A Moral

They come in the night,
And give you a fright,
Right as you turn the lights off.

They don't stop till you wake from sleep,
They make you shout, scream and weep.
They come sometimes,
And fill your head,
So that, tonight, you sleep with dread.

Nightmares love darkness and dread the light,
Reason for this, they stay out of sight.

They are so bold, vivid and real,
Like spiders, scary dolls and broccoli as a meal.

There's beauty in the pain,
Like seeing a live lion's mane,
Sadly, nightmares haunt till you wake,
So pinch yourself, for goodness' sake,
Moral: there is beauty in the pain.

Phoenix Williams (8)
Bandon Hill Primary School, Wallington

The Flying Dinghy

I was navigating the Atlantic
A dinghy I was in
Then my boat sprouted a giant seagull wing
And it was the same the other side!
I was terrified
As the wings started to flap, I realised it wasn't so bad
So I left this world ever so glad

I journeyed the stars of the night sky
I visited a planet made entirely of pie
I grew old in this land
And settled on a planet of sand
Then it all started swirling and mashing
My heart started darting and dashing and...

Pop!

I woke up eleven again
Then I spied a small wall stain
I escaped reality it had seemed
A whole fantastic world I had just dreamed.

Jack Spencer (11)
Bandon Hill Primary School, Wallington

The Day I Entered My Book

Once upon a dream, I entered my book,
It was called The Creakers; if you'd like, have a look.
The book was enchanting and enchanting it was,
To the point where I was in it and I didn't know... because?
Creak! There it was - a creaker right in front of me,
Its large, sinister grin and bright blue eyes as blue as the sea.
It had rough skin and an uneven chewed ear,
Two! Three! More and more started to appear.
I couldn't help but notice them holding a pouch of golden glitter,
They blew it into my face and honestly it tasted quite bitter.
My eyelids grew heavy as I fell asleep,
And that was the end of the constant creak...

Sophie Oguntoyinbo (11)
Bandon Hill Primary School, Wallington

Every Girl's Dream

Have you ever had a dream as a child,
To see unicorns, fairies and things so wild?
Every little girl must have had a dream,
Of a fantasy or unicorns and eating whipped cream,

Have you ever thought of unicorns in another world,
And princesses and fairies that twirled?
The gorgeous, glittering lake,
And when you are awake,
You will be greeted with breakfast in bed,
And slide down mountains on a sled,
And see the shimmering light,
Up in the sky shining very bright,

So have you had a dream like this?
If you did you probably miss,
This phantom and some delightful food,
From a depressed mood to a better mood.

Kexin Luo (10)
Bandon Hill Primary School, Wallington

My Dream About Animals

I woke up with something furry on top of me
To my surprise, a kitty cat was looking down at me
It licked my arm so merrily
Finally, I had enough energy to get up and walk around
I went into my bathroom to see two puppies as cheerful as could be
I hopped down the stairs and saw five lovely bunnies as fluffy as puffy pin clouds
They jumped onto my sofa just like clouds
Time to make breakfast
Into the kitchen I went
I saw three hungry hippos chomping at my fridge
Time to eat
As I sat down in my dining room
All so cosy in my chair
Wait a minute, a deer!
Oh, this wasn't a normal day!
Was I sleeping, dreaming or awake?

Romeesa Khan (9)
Bandon Hill Primary School, Wallington

My Dream

When I am eighteen years old,
I want to work at Disney World,
I want to make kids smile,
They will be happy for a while,
You will never hear someone wail,
In this one-of-a-kind fairy tale,
You will never see someone cry
In this dream of mine.

I realise, when I get there,
It is a thousand times better than a funfair,
I want to be in the parade,
As we say, "Hip, hip hooray!"
People smile and cheer,
And, I can't believe I'm really here,
There is not a better place to be than here,
I see people with Mickey ears,
As we watch to see the fireworks,
I know this is the best place to work.

Florence Macdonald (11)
Bandon Hill Primary School, Wallington

An Unexpected Turn

Once I appeared in an unfamiliar place
In my hand, I saw a case
In front of me, I saw a gingerbread house
Outside it, I saw a mouse
As I walked towards it
To my left, there was a pit
As I strolled through the door
I saw more and more than anything I've seen before
There was more stuff than I would've ever known
And a lot of really expensive cologne
Shelves filled the walls
That looked like they were going to fall
I heard a creak
To my right, there was a leak
In the kitchen, I saw a figure
It was pulling a big trigger
Then he looked at me
And I knew I was in a place I wasn't supposed to be.

Rhys Phillips (10)
Bandon Hill Primary School, Wallington

I Dare Say The Prowling Future

I dare say the prowling future,
It's cautious, waiting for all to land in fixation,
Until it is all done, it awakens its creation,
The devil's work, or God's blessing,
But for now, it lies sleeping,
Come with me, let's take a peeping.

I dare say the present truth,
Please, please help me too. I did nothing, sitting there amused,
It came so fast,
A summer we would never last,
An ever-growing monster, trash mounds,
While heat grows without bounds,
We can't delete trash,
As planet Earth is getting thrashed.

Fight! Fight!
With all your might!
As we await the prowling future.

Anay Nair (10)
Bandon Hill Primary School, Wallington

When I Become A Professional Footballer - The Dream

When I become a professional football player,
I will get skill, another layer,
Goals will be fired in,
I won't be like a bin,
Assists galore,
The crowds roar,
From my perfection,
No deflection,
Needed to score my wonderful goals,
The Champions League, Premier League and World Cup ball rolls,
Last minute, whatever time,
I will be completely sublime,
My talent and creativity,
Won't be a pity,
Football will follow me,
As great as I can be,
I will try harder and harder,
I will succeed farther,

Nothing will make me stop,
Seeing me, fans will acclaim and hop.

Aakash Gandavadi (10)
Bandon Hill Primary School, Wallington

I Dream To Be A Dance Teacher

D ream to be a teacher, not any teacher, a dance teacher.
A nyone can be a dancer or a dance teacher.
N o one should give up.
C an you be a dancer or dance teacher? Yes you can.
E veryone can be a dance teacher or dancer.

T each people how to dance.
E verybody is amazing at dancing.
A nybody can be a dancer or a dance teacher.
C an you be a dancer or dance teacher? Yes.
H ow will you be a dance teacher?
E veryone can be a dance teacher or dancer.
R eally, you or anyone can be a dance teacher or dancer.

Jahmya-Jade Monica Powell (10)
Bandon Hill Primary School, Wallington

My Dreams

When I go to sleep, I swim in the ocean,
Or make a magical potion!
I have dreams where I stand on clouds and breathe the refreshing air,
I never have dreams where I cry in despair!

I have dreams where I fly,
Dreams when I lie,
Dreams where I buy,
And dreams where I'm sky-high!

Until one time when I closed my eyes,
And tons of plant life dies,
People started crying and birds stopped flying,
It gave me such a fright!

The wonderful world of dreams,
Where nothing is what it seems,
While writing this text,
I wonder what will happen next!

Aaron Bijoy (10)
Bandon Hill Primary School, Wallington

The Train Ride

On a dark, stormy night
A steam train powered on with all its might
Up and down big steep hills
Driving past Farmer Bill.

Speeding in and out of tunnels
Steam billowed from its funnels
Skyscrapers went by in a blast
The train ride was going ever so fast.

Coasting along as the river flew
Rocky waters as the strong winds blew
Approaching the village at great velocity
Rain pelting down with a lot of ferocity.

Crash, bam, boom and *smash!*
I woke up sweating in a flash
This terrible hurtling scene
Was all a dream.

Vivaan Mahesh (11)
Bandon Hill Primary School, Wallington

Dreamland

Dreamland is a place where all your dreams come true,
Where everything is made just for you!
If you wish for something you'll get it,
And if you don't go there, you'll regret it!

If you wish, the weather will never be grey,
And you can do anything you wish for all day,
In dreamland everything is fun,
And the endless excitement is never done!

In dreamland, you can eat tons of ice cream
And many thrilling rides will make you scream!
You can go to the beach and play in the sand,
Because these are the amazing possibilities in dreamland.

Sebastian Dixon (11)
Bandon Hill Primary School, Wallington

Nighttime Walk

A boat of your imagination awaits you in your dreams

M ost things in life can be soothed with a walk
O ne thing everyone should know is that you should be yourself
O n a night with a full moon, it is very relaxing to walk a mile
N o matter what, if you look up at the moon, you will see the moon smile

L ove yourself always
I hope one day you will understand the meaning of this poem, you will soon
F orget bad memories and move on
E lectric, sometimes when you have a good day, you'll feel electric.

Nashai Kerr (11)
Bandon Hill Primary School, Wallington

I Have A Dream...

I have a dream,

H elping others no matter what colour they are,
A lways there when someone needs help,
V oices matter, no matter if they are adults or children,
E veryone should be treated equally,

A ll the animals should be saved,

D ozens of people can help with me,
R un the world with care and equality,
E xtremely kind things should fill up everyone's heart,
A ll my love is given to everyone no matter if they are my enemy,
M y dreams must come true in my perfect world.

Disha Sudhakaran (10)
Bandon Hill Primary School, Wallington

My Football Story

I started young so...
Decided that it was my dream
Let's start this story.

I was good at first
But I became way better
So got attention.

In my teenage years
I joined an academy
And I was so close.

But then, I did it
I completed my end goal
But I wanted more.

At 23 I
I won my first Ballon d'Or
This was perfect.

I had a good life
But I won four Ballon d'Ors
In my last four years.

And this is the end
I made everyone so proud
This was so so fun.

Maximus Seear (11)
Bandon Hill Primary School, Wallington

My Dreams

On Christmas Day, in the middle of the night, through the window, a man could be seen. In the middle of the night, he flew over my house and a bang could be heard.

When I went downstairs to see what was happening, I saw a shadow cast on the floor. Then I saw it. Ever so slowly it grew bigger in strength, getting out its legs which were wobbling in the air.

Then I saw its tummy... It was getting closer, coming down the chimney. Then I heard a voice say, "Ho, ho, ho!"

Then, I decided I was dismayed because I was frightened that Father Christmas would do something.

Sheydaen Lahilthan (10)
Bandon Hill Primary School, Wallington

My Nightmare

Me and my sister heard a big, loud roar,
It sounded like a huge wild boar.
Suddenly, lava spurted from a cliff,
We jumped on our scooters, which looked quite stiff.

The lava was catching up, what could we do?
But I started to cry, "Boohoo!"
I started to think,
But I needed to be quick.

The lava got my sister!
And I got a blister!
My parents started to cry,
So did I.

We buried her in a grave,
And there was no rave.
I woke up from my dream,
And went straight back to sleep!

Sebastian Rankin (9)
Bandon Hill Primary School, Wallington

Nightmare Of Monsters

Monsters are in my dream,
They really make me scream,
They are in my head,
They are making me scared,
Whilst I clench myself,
I hope to save myself,
Monsters make me shudder,
And make birds flutter,
My ears ring,
As I hear a ping,
Of those monsters that haunt me,
Whilst I hear the daunting sounds,
Of doom!
But when I wake up, I realise,
I am safely tucked in,
Tucked into my little warm bed,
Without any scary things,
To be heard or said,
So that is the end,
To one big nightmare.

Anay Chaturvedi (10)
Bandon Hill Primary School, Wallington

The Mysteries Of The Galaxy

As I fall into a dream
I am flying in the beautiful night sky
As stars shimmer like diamonds
The moon dances like graceful ballerinas
As many galaxies fly past me, kids below chuckle with a smile
As they slowly turn into delicious candy
My wings break as I drift off into the mysteries of space
Aliens take over as they destroy the galaxy
I'm still here, waiting and waiting for someone or something to come, as I patiently wait
I still feel isolated
I cannot wake from this dream, but I have hope.

Gloria Denovagyte-Valantinaite (9)
Bandon Hill Primary School, Wallington

Kindness

K eep listening
I nclusive
N o mean words
D on't give up
N ice stuff keeps you joyful
E mpower your learning
S eeing all the happy things can keep you calm
S uccess is the plan

I ntelligent
S haring

I nspire
M otivate
P eaceful
O bey the teachers
R esilient
T errific
A mbitious
N ot mean
T ell someone for help.

Abishali Ravinthiran (8)
Bandon Hill Primary School, Wallington

Go High Or Give Up Or Be You

If you go down,
Don't frown,
Just go for the crown,

If the fire burns you up,
Whatever you do, don't give up,

Every spot on your face,
Is beautiful in every place,

You need to believe in yourself,
To get all the trophies on the shelf,

If you don't rock the boat,
You won't get the fish in the moat,

Every hair on your head,
Shows where you sleep in bed,

You are special so don't give up.

Dami Adeyemo (9)
Bandon Hill Primary School, Wallington

Once Upon My Dream

Once upon my dream,
Everybody's glad,
Everybody's playing,
And nobody is sad.

Once upon my dream,
Everybody has shelter,
And as I walk past homes,
I see smiling gnomes.

Once upon my dream,
I see cheery animals eating food,
And all that I can tell,
Is that nobody is in a bad mood.

Once upon my dream,
I look outside and see bright flowers,
When I look to the other side,
I see children with small powers.

Samanvi Nagasri Vadlamudi (11)
Bandon Hill Primary School, Wallington

A Frightful Nightmare

Ever had a fright?
About a clown, spider
Or vampire in the night
Maybe you got out of your parents' sight
And now you are lost

You try to fight it
But you know it will cost you your life
So you start to run away
Because you see it pull out a knife!

Ever had a fright?
About dying, drowning
Or getting locked out your house at night?
Maybe a ghost is using your kite
But you know better than to fight.

Emilia Tett (11)
Bandon Hill Primary School, Wallington

My Dream House

In my world of dreams,
The skies are sapphire blue,
The houses are made of food,
And there is an ecstatic mood,
My house is made of bacon and waffles,
All the people stand baffled there,
Their mouths watering, sweating everywhere.
Though they haven't seen the jelly bean pool,
They are excited to eat it all,
The gummy bears chase them away,
You shall never come again, they say,
So I can relax and play.

Ella Sorel (10)
Bandon Hill Primary School, Wallington

What A Nightmare

Demons and monsters surrounding me,
I am like a little flea,
Along the dark, dreadful street,
Monsters coming in a fleet.

I am an iceberg, extremely cold,
My attempt at being bold
Is in vain,
I cannot bear the pain.

Walking with a sudden *thud*,
Reality rushing back to me like a flood,
I cannot comprehend this!
My mind was an empty abyss,
Why couldn't I remember anything?

Nikhil Nibu Kuriakose (11)
Bandon Hill Primary School, Wallington

A Perfect World

Clear skies, no pollution,
That's my perfect world.
Where differences are okay,
That's my perfect world.
No litter, clear roads,
That's my perfect world.
Where everyone's appearances are okay,
That's my perfect world.
No negatives,
That's my perfect world.
Where my voice is heard,
That's my perfect world.
Where my dreams come true,
That's my perfect world...

Isla Lacey (10)
Bandon Hill Primary School, Wallington

The Importance Of Attitude

I can't do it
I won't listen to people who say
I can do it
It's true that
I won't achieve anything
It's not right that
I will do it
Giving up is the right thing
It's not at all true that
I can handle this
It's right to say that
I will not be able to do it
It's not correct that
I can do it

Read this from bottom to top for a change of attitude.

Zeynab Kafizas (10)
Bandon Hill Primary School, Wallington

Nightmare

N ightmares took place last night
I then ended up waking with a fright
G ot to end this curse
H ippogriffs came soaring as things became worse
T he tremendously steep hill led to a haunted house
M ightily, I entered the house while I was a silent mouse
A fter, I was hit with a hammer on the head
R oughly dragged into a peculiar shed
E nded up awake in bed.

Reshmi Ramamoorthi (10)
Bandon Hill Primary School, Wallington

Nightmares

N ighttime sky fuels the worry
I get into my bed and fall asleep
G etting to sleep seems impossible
H aving nightmares in my sleep
T errifying and scary, it makes me weep
M y bed is uncomfortable
A nd I see a monster in my sleep
R acing a monster in my dream
E lectric feeling in my veins in a good way
S cared and terrified, I wake up in my bed.

Blake Turner (10)
Bandon Hill Primary School, Wallington

Papaya

Romeo's Papaya cat,
What a beautiful cat!
My best friend brought it to school,
And I thought it was really cool!
Me just looking at the dread,
But after just looking at the cat which looked like bread!
Just an animal with innocent pink paws,
But having giant claws.
Who doesn't like cats?
Well, maybe just stinky rats.
Oh no! Romeo dropped Papaya!
I'm joking, I'm just a liar...

Zainab Munawar (9)
Bandon Hill Primary School, Wallington

Once Upon A...

D azzling mermaids riding on unicorns feeding cats and leading them to the palace.
R iding underwater unicorns to find treasure and pretty pearls to measure the glittering treasure.
E ating rainbow shells, drinking the pink milk of magical cows.
A t the bright night, we act out animals that live underwater.
M eeting more beautiful mermaids, starlight cats and rainbow unicorns with shimmery tales.

Shirley Guo (7)
Bandon Hill Primary School, Wallington

The Haunted House In My Nightmare

I had a nightmare yesterday
That I saw a creepy man on the bay,
He said to me, "Come and follow me if you dare,"
So I ran away like a scared hare,
Then I arrived at the forest,
Then I glared at a terrifying florist,
He banished,
But I suddenly vanished,
I came upon a haunted house,
Where I saw a massive mouse,
I ran away in fright,
Then I saw a beaming light...

Kerem Colak (10)
Bandon Hill Primary School, Wallington

My Desire With God

I turn out to be a Jehovah's Witness,
You do not need fitness to be a witness.
Be the best person for God,
Be sensible, he does not need bars of gold.
Spread the word, for God's kingdom to come,
I want to go there, it will be our new home.
Become a witness, it is the best,
Make friends, more is not less.
Exercise faith, this is the way,
In order to keep our previous stay.

Milo Cheng (10)
Bandon Hill Primary School, Wallington

Horse Riding

H ome away from home
O ff hacking
R oad walks back from the field
S chooling horses
E legant horses.

R iding your favourite horse
I n a muddy field falling over
D inner for the horse, better than Gordon Ramsay
I n the school, leading the lesson kids
N o horses walking nicely
G rooming before a ride.

Elsie Noble (11)
Bandon Hill Primary School, Wallington

My Football Career

When I was nine, I wanted to quit gymnastics, and eventually, when I was ten I did, but then I did what I truly wanted to do, which is football.
When I was ten and a half, I joined a football team. I started in goal, thinking that is what I wanted to do but then I was in defence and worked my way up to midfield. Now I am eleven, I have three medals.
One day I will be a lioness, bringing home the gold.

Penny Polley (11)
Bandon Hill Primary School, Wallington

My Dreamland

D elicious doughnut trees
R unaway gummy bears escaping
E verywhere there are sweet treats
A mazing snacks everywhere I look
M arvellous mouth-watering macarons
L ollipop ladies walking on rainbow roads
A ncient biscuits being visited by marshmallow men
N o vegetables in this land
D oughnut wake me from this dream.

Lara Suvari (10)
Bandon Hill Primary School, Wallington

If I Were The Mayor Of London

If I were the Mayor of London, I would fix all the train derailments and train cancellations. I would give everyone more bank holidays. On the weekends, everyone would have free travel and would get an ice cream of their choice. I would also give everyone free lemonade and Fanta.

At 11:59pm on New Year's Eve, I will gather everyone near Big Ben and everyone will shout, "Happy New Year!"

Sonny Mistry (10)
Bandon Hill Primary School, Wallington

A Dreadful Dream

Having to think about unwanted creatures,
Without knowing any of their features,
Crawling through the night,
With a battle of fright,
Just thinking and thinking,
In the absence of twitching and blinking,
Terror of being caught by it tonight,
That made me cry, which blurred my sight,
Who knows, I could be under threat,
And could also end up being dead.

Pragya Bhadani (11)
Bandon Hill Primary School, Wallington

Once Upon A...

A vatar called Aang and Korra
V oids galore, portals galore, only those in sight
A ang and Korra blasting with might, Sokka and me watching with amazement
T hey use their strong powers, Aang air and Korra water
A ang uses all his might, blasting Korra with all his strength
R un, Korra, quickly, into a portal, closed when she got there.

Mawuena Badasu (7)
Bandon Hill Primary School, Wallington

Injury

I once had a dream,
As weird as can be.
I was with my friends,
The night would never end,
Then suddenly came,
A dance move of fame.
Rodger and Rose were partners,
Then suddenly came an unexpected turn.
Rodger broke his leg,
Then he started to beg.
The paramedics came,
They said all was okay,
Rodger said, "Hooray!"

Evelyn Nkrumah (9)
Bandon Hill Primary School, Wallington

Once Upon A

D azzling disco balls on the ceiling with dancing dogs all over the place.
R ainbow stars all in the air, like a singing mermaid.
E ngaging fairies with a cat right beneath their feet.
A mazing, beautiful princesses and queens that love to sing and dance.
M elting ice cream in a candy shop, oh so far the king couldn't reach.

Isla Summerfield (7)
Bandon Hill Primary School, Wallington

Nightmares

Something's chasing me,
What could it be?
Something is coming for me!

Could it be a monster?
Could it be a murderer?
Could it be my friends who betrayed me?

Nightmares!
They make you run and scream!
Nightmares!
Until you wake from your dream!
Nightmares!
What is this mystery?
How does this
Happen in your head?

Aahan Nath (10)
Bandon Hill Primary School, Wallington

Cricket

C atch the ball to get someone out
R un and win runs by hitting a four or a six
I n a match, play well to win the game
C ricket is all about having fun and enjoying your time
K icking the ball is not ideal and will hurt
E at lightly before any match
T rick opponents so that you can have the advantage.

Shri Sankalp Maryala (11)
Bandon Hill Primary School, Wallington

Daring To Dream

The doctor was in a room then suddenly, he drank a potion. He started to sleep. He became an evil doctor and he found a diamond. The doctor spread a virus which made people turn into monsters.
Six humans survived and they needed to stop the virus. Too late. He invented more terrible horror monsters. "We need to stop Doctor Who and the diamond!"

Piero Jara Ortega (7)
Bandon Hill Primary School, Wallington

Why Me, Why Me, Why Me?

I look inside my mind
N ightmare
S inging clouds
I 'm going insane
D on't ask
E ach night

M y mind is blown
Y ou'll never understand

M ore of it
I t's insane
N ever do this again
D on't, just don't.

Josh Hyland (9)
Bandon Hill Primary School, Wallington

Dream World

D reaming of a better world,
R unning on orange grass,
E ating as much as you want,
A iding as many people as you can,
M eeting dream people,

W aking up disorientated,
O pen your eyes,
R ealise it was a dream,
L ooking for your dream friends
D ream on.

Charlie Nicol (11)
Bandon Hill Primary School, Wallington

Don't Fight It (Nightmare)

Ssss... spiders crawling up your back
Circle with a dot,
Blood gushing down your throat
X marks the spot.
Follow the path
Arrive at your bath,
Laugh while you drown
Into the shadow night.
Bloody Mary's skeleton
Monsters under your bed,
Cockroaches in your pillowcase
Grenades blowing up a cake.

Saraneya Arulmugan (9)
Bandon Hill Primary School, Wallington

Nightmares

They come in the night as soon as you turn off the light
Nightmares come and fill your head
Making your sleep full of dread
They can be scary if you're not wary
Make sure you're prepared if you're really scared
Nightmares come and haunt your dreams
But it seems like you're unseen
In your very own dream...

Tanatswa Taruvamba (9)
Bandon Hill Primary School, Wallington

I Have A Dream

I have a dream,
That I want to be on a professional football team,
Where I shine,
Where I will spend all of my time,

I have a dream,
Where I will try my best,
And do no less,

I have a dream,
That the football pitch is my stage,
And I play in front of people at a young age,

I have a dream.

Libby Roberts (9)
Bandon Hill Primary School, Wallington

A Small Disaster

It first started at a small camp,
Then it was very damp,
The earthquake destroyed the lands,
And glass cut my hands.
The fire burned the town,
And someone stole the king's crown.
The tornado had destroyed the mice,
I felt like I was in ice.
There was a spider on my head,
And I realised I was in my bed.

Umar Najimudeen (9)
Bandon Hill Primary School, Wallington

Premier League

One cup, one dream,
Desire to win the league,
Best players in the best league,
Who will win the league?
The best teams trying to win again,
The worst teams trying to avoid relegation,
The players with big dreams,
Managers trying to make their dreams the best,
The fans are happy when they go on a winning streak.

Ali Khan (10)
Bandon Hill Primary School, Wallington

Dreaming Of Football

I have a dream, I want to be a footballer
Join a club and play my best
And do no less.

Everybody can play
Boys and girls
Every single day.

I have a dream, I want to be a footballer
To be the top defender in every match
To be captain of my team
And dream till it comes true.

Tori Trinidad (10)
Bandon Hill Primary School, Wallington

A Mad Dream

I go to bed,
Then I see a beautiful land before me
I cannot believe my eyes
There is a table full of pies
I start to stuff my face,
These pies are ace.
Then it looms over me,
A great big hornet bee
I scream, I shout
It starts raining cream.
Then I woke up,
It was all a dream.

Sidney Devereux-Gent (9)
Bandon Hill Primary School, Wallington

I Dream

I dream of good things and getting noticed.

D reams are good, we get ideas, we think.
R eal, your dreams could come true, be *big*.
E veryone has dreams, sometimes they are good or bad.
A dream is wonderful, it helps you sleep.
M y dreams are wonderful.

Thomas Banks (10)
Bandon Hill Primary School, Wallington

The Time I Was In Hell

One time I was in hell,
I walked to Tartarus and almost fell.
The field of punishment always had hail,
Everyone was always pale.
I rode on the aerobus,
It was nothing like a normal bus.
Then I woke up and found out it was a dream,
And now I know I don't want to be on the hell team.

Jeremy Qin (8)
Bandon Hill Primary School, Wallington

Out Of This World

My night was amazing
I was out of this world with animals flying around me
It was out of this world!
I saw unicorns and birds as we flew about
It was too good to be true, almost.
The moon was bright
The stars were shining
The sun was going up
It was shining as the moon went down.

Aria Cleghorn (7)
Bandon Hill Primary School, Wallington

Nightmare

They come in the night
As soon as you turn off the light
Nightmares come and fill your head
Making you sleep, full of dread.

If you are not scared of blood
Then you must like most nightmares
Do you like having nightmares?
It feels dreadful being haunted by nightmares.

Krishnujan Kannathasan (9)
Bandon Hill Primary School, Wallington

My Puppy World

When my puppies are out of stock,
I go to my puppy block.
I press the button with a shiver,
And out come all the little mutters.
Each time I listen very carefully,
I hear a squeak inside a treat.
Each mile I see a pile
Of puppies in a puddle with a smile.

Miya Cheng (8)
Bandon Hill Primary School, Wallington

Once Upon A...

D ay, I saw Disneyland and there was Mickey Mouse dancing in a disco. I was
R iding on a roller coaster, then I was
E ating some delicious, gold, huge gummy bears
A nd it was the most fantastic day -
M ickey and Minnie Mouse, amazing!

Jaiwin Kalaicheivan (7)
Bandon Hill Primary School, Wallington

Dreams

D reams improve your imagination.
R eality is my dream.
E xploring the worlds of darkness and brightness.
A dream can take you as far as you want.
M y dreams are my wishes.
S ometimes, they are wishes for both you and me.

Jasper Liem (11)
Bandon Hill Primary School, Wallington

Once Upon A...

D azzling, dancing dogs at a dancing club
R ainbow, fluffy unicorns wrapping lots of presents
E ating cheesy pasta but the cat doesn't like it
A magical fairy riding a cute bird
M aking a yummy banana cake for a monkey.

Esin Vaid (7)
Bandon Hill Primary School, Wallington

Dream

D ancing football players, wow!
R apping birds flying and raining blue, eating crisps
E agles are there, just eating
A mazing cheetah was looking at delicious food
M agical dog is the king of the land, he was so happy.

Bentley Good (7)
Bandon Hill Primary School, Wallington

What Am I?

I can be as imaginative as anything,
You can only see me at night,
If you are nocturnal, you see me at daytime,
I might give you a fright or inspire you,
You can't control me, I am random,
What am I?

Answer: A dream.

Milan Patel (9)
Bandon Hill Primary School, Wallington

What Are Nightmares? What Is A Dream?

What is a dream?
Is it where you go for a ride?
Is it when you swim in the ocean?
Or even a magical potion?
Is it meant to scare you awake?
Or to drift you off far away...
Does it make you smile or scream?
What really is a dream?

Samantha Adielle Magesh (10)
Bandon Hill Primary School, Wallington

Once Upon A Dream

D izzy donkeys sit on a fluffy comfy sofa.
R olling rats making a mess.
E nchanted princesses dancing around the palace.
A red grassy apple was lying on the floor,
M ermaids floating in the glistening, calm sea.

Isha Nayak (7)
Bandon Hill Primary School, Wallington

The Golden Knight

I've heard about a golden knight,
He comes to me every night,
Clitter-clatter, see his horse,
As it runs, speaking Morse.

He fights devils,
And destroys perils,
And if he was dead,
I'd jump out of bed!

Mithulan Pirabaharan (8)
Bandon Hill Primary School, Wallington

Dream

D reams are imaginary
R emind yourself of your dreams because they can be true
E very day you have unexpected dreams
A s you dream you have a beam of sunlight inside
M any dreams are a grin in your sleep.

Yago Bañuelos (9)
Bandon Hill Primary School, Wallington

Untitled

D isney is really exciting for people.
R ainy days for witches who are scary.
E ating tasty food for unicorns.
A mber dancing unicorns that are rapping.
M oving, grooving monkeys in a disco.

Livvy Griscti (7)
Bandon Hill Primary School, Wallington

Untitled

My dream is to go to Japan
To see the pink cherry blossoms
And the beautiful trees
Every time I see, it feels like I am in another world
To see the big cities that are like mazes
The calm streams rushing by.

Nathanael Mullings
Bandon Hill Primary School, Wallington

Fulham

F ulham is the best word
U p and down Fulham go
L ose and win
H undreds of fans shouting my name
A fan always wants to be seen
M illions of fans support them.

Tilly Turner (10)
Bandon Hill Primary School, Wallington

Untitled

D izzy dinosaurs in a world of chaos,
R ockets rumbling,
E ating an enchanted meal
A mighty rock speeding to the moon
M agical, magnificent mansions appear.

Filip Grabowski (7)
Bandon Hill Primary School, Wallington

Once Upon A...

D elicious chocolate with
R ainbow sprinkles
E ating the delicious chocolate
A ggressively eating delicious chocolate
M unching up the scrumptious chocolate.

Lucas Mackin (7)
Bandon Hill Primary School, Wallington

Dream Land

D elicious snacks
R eal, is it or not?
E verywhere are amazing snacks
A nd some sweets wherever I look
M arvellous marshmallows everywhere and anywhere.

Poppy Baldwin (10)
Bandon Hill Primary School, Wallington

Once Upon A...

D ancing Disney characters
R ainbows and puppies dancing on the Disney floor
E ating sparkling crisps
A ll the Disney guests
M y birthday party is here.

Katie Duke (7)
Bandon Hill Primary School, Wallington

Horrible Hell

Something is in front of me
It looks like it's mean
What could it be?
Many things surround me in my brain
And it's walking on me
A mini murderer and a devil.

Kristian Wilkins (9)
Bandon Hill Primary School, Wallington

The Ocean

The beautiful ocean,
But sometimes not,
Sunken ships stay there a lot,
Litter fills the oceans,
Because of us,
Please save our oceans,
And join us.

Oscar Saunders (10)
Bandon Hill Primary School, Wallington

Fairies

Faster and faster my heart pumped. I couldn't believe what I saw.
Above a tree stood a magnificent creature. A fairy, after all.
I was stunned. It was almost like I was frozen in place
As she looked me in the eyes and gave me a gaze.
The ringing of a bell I heard, then, *poof!*
She was gone. I was confused.
I couldn't remember a thing about her. All I remembered was her mystical, glittering smile that could heal any wound
Her eyes that, inside, would have probably looked like a lush field
And her antique, fragile wings that looked like they would blow away in a brush of wind.
Enchanting thoughts filled my head that night when I went to bed.
Was it my imagination or something I'd read?
Since that day, I still don't know the answer.
Who knows what the future holds for me?
Even if I don't see her again, I still go to that tree,
Hoping for the best. I guess today is my lucky day
As I get to see her again.

Mollie Baca Jackson (9)
Cippenham Primary School, Slough

A Day With Your Teacher

A day with your teacher is the best day ever.

D ay after day, you are with your teacher to sit and play.

A day when you're skipping in a field with blooming flowers.

Y et another day having a picnic in a peaceful park.

W hen you're alone, you have someone there like your teacher.

I f I feel scared, I go to my teacher, it feels the best.

T he day you feel good, you take your teacher for an adventure.

H owever, if you feel sad, give your teacher a hug, and no more tears.

Y ou go on adventures with your teacher, you are adventurous.

O ne day, together having fun playing with your teacher's dog, yes please.

U s in the house, baking a special recipe, made with love.

R eading on the bed with your favourite book in your hand, and your teacher next to you.

T he day you grow up, you will remember the best teacher ever.
E very time something happens, you have someone to go to.
A time when you're hurt, you will always have a buddy.
C an't think about bad things when you're around your amazing teacher.
H aunted by something, no need to worry, just hold your teacher's hand.
E ven when the day ends, a new day will begin, to meet her again.
R esting on the beach after a busy day with your super teacher.

Julia Wenderlich (10)
Cippenham Primary School, Slough

Nightmares Of Voices

In the land of dreams where shadows play
Nightmares of voices come out to stay
Whispering secrets, eerie and strange
In a haunting melody that makes us deranged
They emerge from the darkness unseen and sly
With whispers that make your heart sigh
Their words are like riddles, puzzling and deep
A mystery to unravel before we sleep
Nightmares of voices, oh what a fright
But let's explore this eerie night
For within the darkness, there is much to learn
In the realm of dreams where fantasies churn
The voices may taunt, but we won't despair
We'll face them bravely with courage to spare
With every word they speak, we'll find a clue
To unlock the secrets and make dreams come true
In the realm of nightmares, we'll unravel the plot
And turn their haunting whispers into a knot
For even in darkness there is always light
To guide us through the shadows of the night
So fear not the nightmares, let's embrace the chase
And discover the wonders hidden in space

Nightmares of voices, a puzzle to solve
In dreams we will triumph and forever evolve.

Arsh Pannu (10)
Cippenham Primary School, Slough

Monster

M onsters everywhere, under your bed, and even maybe in your hair as you shave it all off.
O nly smart monsters sit on hair, and if you find hair and glasses on your chair, you know who has been there.
N ever, ever let a monster inside, even if they look like your uncle with horns.
S o, if you happen to let a monster in, distract it by giving it tea, then put a doughnut outside. When the monster goes out for it, close the door.
T ea is a great distraction for monsters, because they love it, but they hate Brussels sprouts.
E ven if a monster goes under your bed, just put a Brussels sprout under there. It will be gone within one to ten seconds.
R emember, stay far, far, far away from monsters even if they look like your mum.

Michael Amery
Cippenham Primary School, Slough

Why Should I Get Involved, I'm Popular?

They cornered Harry against the locker
They abused him verbally and physically
They threw him to the polished ground
Why should I get involved
I'm popular?

Atif was cornered at the back of the fields
Repulsive slurs and punches were dished out
On the emerald grass he lay for a while
Why should I get involved
I'm popular?

They grabbed Jakub out of the lunch hall
Those animals beat him, soft like a sponge
In a corner he lay reflecting on the malicious abuse dealt to him
Why should I get involved
I'm popular?

On my way home
Four hooded people circled around me
I was never there to help
Now no one was around to help me.

Aariya Mistry (9)
Cippenham Primary School, Slough

A Circus Dream

In my super cool dream, dragons were the main stars of the circus show
Breathing fire, making the whole place glow
Their shiny scales in all colours of the rainbow
In my dragon dream, that stole the show
Juggling with their tails flying up so high
In this awesome dragon circus, reaching for the sky
It was like a magical adventure with dragons ruling the air
In my dream circus, nothing could compare!
The dragons danced gracefully
Their wings creating a magical breeze
In a spectacular display that brought everyone to their knees
The crows cheered and clapped
Amazed by the dragon's fiery might
In that dream circus, it was a mesmerising sight.

Musa Talib (10)
Cippenham Primary School, Slough

My Dream: Flying

F lying through the withered winds, eyeing the vast expanse of the horizon.
L ovely sky that reminds me of my family and the ones I hold so dear.
Y ears seem to go by, listening to the sound of the trickling water, joined with the voices of birds.
I n the night, flying high, there's a beacon of light guiding me to my destiny.
N ew memories I make, whilst flying high and looking down at my house - my home - my life.
G liding through the night, my dream comes to an end, while the sun gazes down at our wonderful world.

Sunny Singh Johal (10)
Cippenham Primary School, Slough

Wizards And Shadows

Once upon a time,
There was a wizard
Called Zane. Zane
Would regularly
Wish he had someone
Like him to talk with.

It never happened
Though... One time,
Zane found a
Black silhouette
Just as the
Sky brightened up.

He named it
Shadow, his
Best friend.
Every time
He realised
Something.

Shadow couldn't
Talk. Zane mixed tiger hair and lime
Juice and dumped

Them on his shadow. A few
Swirls, then Shadow began talking.

Alfie Webb (10)
Cippenham Primary School, Slough

Future Dream

Firstly, I wake up
Up to drink milk in my cup
To be sacrificed and killed
Unsatisfactory, I'd rather be climbing a hill
Right, I'm in bed
End it. There is nothing to worry about in my head.

Damn, can't believe it
Right after I say it, I fall into the pit
The pit makes me die
Die, die and fly
To be sacrificed the day before
Not what you would want!

That day, I make a plot
That doesn't work
But helps a lot
So that's the plot
That made me suffer a lot.

Benyamin Fiotmane (10)
Cippenham Primary School, Slough

Trapped In A Dragon's Cage!

When the clock strikes midnight, the dragon's eye will play I Spy. He will travel. He will also spy, but he will have to hide!
He leaves the place to play a dragon's game. He arrives at last at the dragon's planet. He sees the beast looking for its prey.
Humans.
He has been seen. The fireball kills his light. Its feet can be seen. The dragon's eyes follow him like the moon orbiting a dead end – one that will surely mean death. He is eaten and never seen again.

Ibrahim Butt (9)
Cippenham Primary School, Slough

My BFF

Be like a flower, don't race to first place, don't be a tall tower, don't be a beast, we're all the most, the most amazing.

We shared every tear
We felt each other's fear
Like a moon, she lights up the dark
Situations you're always there
For me when I need you
You always make me feel more
Confident
Never leaving my side, you're as beautiful
As ocean tides, we go on emotional rides
You love me
I love you too.

Zoha Ihsan (9)
Cippenham Primary School, Slough

Sweet Dreams

As I woke, I was in a land full of marshmallows.
I said to myself, "Where am I?"
I remembered dreaming about marshmallows.
So I walked around and saw a white, gloomy figure
Dancing in the moonlight.
I got closer, but then it disappeared.
So I walked more and saw fogs of colour.
I tried touching one and *whoosh*,
When I woke up, it was night, and my mum was in my room saying, "Sweet dreams."

Maya Deliu (10)
Cippenham Primary School, Slough

Summer

S ummer is fun, especially out in the sun.
U nder the sun, you dream, go and get your ice cream.
M y house is a bore; let's play out ashore.
M any people are a smarty, so our friends can have a party.
E veryone will go to the pool, where the sun shines like a jewel.
R ecess is here, so let's have a cheer.

Saimaathmika Prasad (10)
Cippenham Primary School, Slough

Sneak Future Peek

I haven't seen the place before,
A million winged beasts in the core.
I feel scared, unusual, insecure,
Like some ants being lured.

I look around for Enders, as they only come in stones,
But all I could see was skinny bones.
With wearing party hats and party cones,
I gave up, but until next year, in my gaming prime.

Kushank Saini (10)
Cippenham Primary School, Slough

Lost

Lost in the mysterious bogs,
Pixies resting on the vibrant logs,
Pesky pixies, flying away,
As they landed on the magical bay,
I'm wondering around in the midnight forest,
Near the tree which is the proudest,
I'm lost in the magical forest,
I can't get out, no matter how hard I try.

Arsal Nasir (10)
Cippenham Primary School, Slough

Dreams

D reams hold adventures of the mind,
R emarkable adventures you will find,
E xciting adventures out at sea,
A dventures of the world being the size of your knee,
M aking stories left and right,
S eeing dreams with beauty and light.

Rahma Bouzid (10)
Cippenham Primary School, Slough

A Mystical World

Every night I go to bed
And mystical dreams go through my head
I see a wizard cast a spell
And throw a penny in a well
With a swish
He makes a wish
A dragon sat so smooth and shiny
Appears before me but it is quite tiny.

Noah Heath
Cippenham Primary School, Slough

What Is That Under My Bed?

What is that under my bed?
Is it a monster eating some pasta
Or a lobster looking in my cluster of teddy bears
because I don't know!

Or a huge monster using my unicorn duster to itch its
back in a box!
Or even worse, two monsters saying I am a better
boxer than you and going to fight

Ahh! There is thunder outside my room
And something under my bed
What can I do? I hope this is a joke
Or am I dreaming and having a nightmare?

But I am not dreaming a nightmare
This is real, just face it
But they can chase me I can see it
So just look under with the thunder

Phew! It is James
"James, are you playing online games? Because your room floor is carpet and mine is wooden and yours is so soft!"
Aya!
What is that under my bed?

Sofia Jivani (8)
Glebe Primary School, Kenton

The Football Of Doom

Once upon a time, there was a little boy called Jack, and he always loved football. His favourite player was Messi, but his mum always said his room was messy. His mum said, "Do you want to go to a football club?" Then Jack screamed in excitement, and of course, he said yes.

When it was the first day of Jack's football club, he did not know what to do until one of the coaches asked him if he needed help. Jack said, "Yes!" And when it was match time, he was scoring goal after goal. No one could stop him.

Even when he was a goalie, he still scored, but in the last second, it was tied 7-7, but there was a penalty for the opposing team, and if they scored, they would win the trophy. But Jack saved it and shot it from range, and... *Boosh!* It went into the goal, and they won.

Jayan Hirani (8)
Glebe Primary School, Kenton

Dinosaurs

D o you ever wonder what would happen if dinosaurs were not extinct?
I f you do, these are the good things that may happen.
N o way would you be able to ride on a T-rex, but you may be able to go on a small one!
O h, I forgot, you may be able to ride a dinosaur to school!
S o these are the good things that may happen!
A nd here are the bad things that might happen.
U nless it is a small dinosaur, it might crush your house if it stomps on it!
R ight, now, I've suggested the things that may or may not happen.
S o, this is the end of a poem for dinosaur dreams.

Aarish Morani (8)
Glebe Primary School, Kenton

Epic Dancer

E nd of the day, start of the night,
P eople start to feel a little bit of fright.
I , however, am ready for dreams!
C inderella might come, I greet her with an ice cream.

D ancer, I see a dancer, she is gorgeous,
A s beautiful as the sun, she dances.
N ot anyone is heard, but we all glance.
C rystal drooping, she is like, all plain and white
E veryone gives a round of applause, I am totally inspired - when I grow up, an athlete I might just be...!
R ight, I shall be anyone, can do anything, just wait, you'll see! Then I wake up too.

Mahi Shah (8)
Glebe Primary School, Kenton

I Had A Dream

Dream, dream, dream,
I had a dream that I was a famous superstar,
I was driving a big silver car.
I was singing songs at a concert,
I had a very tasty dessert.
I met lots of celebrities,
They had kind personalities.
I was signing autographs,
People were taking photographs.
I was watching some movies,
I had many duties.
I bought anything I want,
I bought an elephant, I named him Kant.
I stuffed my face with ice cream
And burgers.
But then I woke up and realised it was just a dream…
And I'm hungry for some ice cream!

Elisabeth Toma (8)
Glebe Primary School, Kenton

The Queen's Dream

The Queen's dream will spark tonight,
Her dreams are very bright,
She stares at the stars,
Right next to all the cars,
Dreaming, dreaming with magic beaming,
She went back inside and started cleaning,
Before she went to bed she saw the velvet sky,
In the morning before she woke up,
She saw a rainbow,
She put on her bow,
Getting ready to start the day,
With a lovely play,
She was ready to have a sing-song,
Roll along,
She made some marshmallow smores,
Getting ready to snore.

Kiyana Patel (8)
Glebe Primary School, Kenton

Puppies

I was wandering about in the massive alleyway and right as I was about to leave, I saw not two, not three but five cute, little puppies. They were adorable.
I made a great choice and took the puppies home. It was hard work taking care of the puppies. I named them Turbo, Nubby, Rover, Tayo and Charlie.
It was very fun taking care of these tiny puppies, though unfortunately, one of my best friends is taking them home soon so I need to love them so much before my friend takes them.

Aaditya Rathod (7)
Glebe Primary School, Kenton

Magic Land

Wandering around like a flying bee, I reach Magic Land
Oh look what I see, a tree with lots of jelly that's good for my belly,

The flow in the chocolate river has a magical glow,
We slide through the colourful rainbow,

We hide in a bush and push some berries,
Look! We see some corn in a horn,

Let's go for a new adventure

See you there.

Aahana Sahai (7)
Glebe Primary School, Kenton

Starry Night

A starry night
Its stars are so bright
The shiny moon
With a wonderful gloom
The Northern Lights
What a wonderful sight
A shooting star
Probably a protein bar
The moon is crescent
Which is pleasant

The shiny stars
I can barely see Mars
It's magic in the sky
It catches my eyes
What a starry night.

Tiana Rabadia (8)
Glebe Primary School, Kenton

The Fairies

Fairies are fun, fairies are joy, fairies are helpful, even kind,
Fairies dance under the bright, shiny sky.
Fairies are magic,

Fairies are fun, fairies are joy, fairies are helpful, even kind,
Fairies dance under the bright, shiny sky.
Fairies are magic, magic, magic!

Krisha Jayswal (8)
Glebe Primary School, Kenton

My Dream!

I went and had some food with my friend, Hannah. We were going to sing and dance. I hoped people would smile like the sun! I was so excited.

When we were going, the sun and wind danced. Then we realised we didn't do some moving exercise. I raced back like Hannah was. When we were stretching, there was a crack, we bent our fingers. As usual, we wrote books before the dance show.

We went into the car and we zoomed. When we got there, I saw the strawberry Loveheart on top of the building and there was a Loveheart sweet, lots of them, for the walls.

We went in, there was a crash. It was the bin, it fell over. We went into our costumes. When we went out, we saw a light spotlight on my family and my cousins and sister.

Eevee Brookes (8)
Gunter Primary School, Pype Hayes

To Live By The Sandy Beach...

The gold, sandy sand, dancing and hopping with lots of joy.
The green, long seaweed is swishing and swashing.
The big waves are as loud as a lion's roar.
The crystal blue, wavy water, washing up on the sandy beach.
The sky is as blue as the ocean.

Everyone on the beach is as bright as the sun.
On the palm trees, the coconuts taste like the best drink ever, it left me in shock!
The fish are dancing and jumping in the air.
The dolphins are singing and floating on top of the water.
The shark is floating around on the water as still as a statue.
All of the fish are laughing with laughter and jumping like a human would do.

There is a fish, in a dish. It tastes like real fish but it's made out of candy. A candy fish!

Look, there is Cristiano Ronaldo on the beach! He kicks the ball into the goal. It makes a *bang*! It is so powerful that the floor is shaking and an earthquake almost erupted.

It's time to go to bed, so I head to sleep in my villa.
The next morning, we go back to the beach and we have a fantastic time!

Romé Hamilton (8)
Gunter Primary School, Pype Hayes

Insane Kpop Timeline

Trapped in a strong cube it goes *boom, boom*
Suddenly, the power of fart lets me out of despair by the room
In 2011 as crowded as a concert
I go growl as I have money to insert
Back at my house with my kind mother
Watching K-dramas; I'm jealous that I don't have a brother
2013, fizz whizz my nightmare
I need to obtain my dream somehow
I try to get out like a speedy hare

Oh no, I get robbed
This means only one thing, I'm the robber this time
13 squirrels, I adore them all
Bouncy Bob, Hungry Harold and Shopping Mall
I join the pup club, all dogs red
Nick, Pam and unfortunately the last one is dead
Playing Mario, I'm a sweaty, energetic gamer
I rage quit like a pro though, I love cutting paper
I am a pirate now, I see pigs with a dirty gaze
In District 9, I bring out a daily praise.

I'm in town with my friends going aargh
Seeing a Charizard with ma chickens
My favourite energy store is closed, nooooo
I sneak through the back door, oh, ho, ho, ho
In high school, hard GCSEs and tests
I'm really mad, my food's a mess
Now a police officer, great at the job
Case 143 at the pace of a mop.

Aidan Ly (9)
Gunter Primary School, Pype Hayes

Billie Eilish Concert

My dream is to go to a Billie Eilish concert
Her hair is as green as grass and black as the night sky
I went to see her at her concert
She danced on the stage as if she were a snowflake
She looked very classy
The spotlight hit and shone on her as if she were a star
I felt happier than ever when she asked me on stage
When I heard her I fell to the ground
A bit of stagefright struck my bones when I got on stage
The crowd was staring intently at me and I felt nervous
When I sang on stage, I sang my favourite song
The crowd jumped to its feet and roared in appreciation
When I stopped, people begged for another song
I asked Billie Eilish and she said yes so I sang my second favourite song
My parents cheered me on constantly
The crowd cheered me on and asked for another song but I said I couldn't possibly stay
They begged and begged me, I couldn't take it so said fine and I said this would be the last song
After I finished there was a thud on the stage

I passed out and found myself at home
I woke up, home sweet home.

Arabella Swan Jones (8)
Gunter Primary School, Pype Hayes

The Demiverse

I wake up in my world,
It's hard to see in this fog,
Deep into the darkness of outer space,
It's a weird kind of place.

Bang! Bang! Smash! I crash,
I fall in a hole,
I land on a bowl,
A clown tries to catch me,
But I try to be me.

Suddenly, I have to pee,
But where is that going to be?
I think I am in a nightmare,
I am going on a highway.

I see a car,
Boom! I get run over,
It is carnage,
I need a bandage,
I see a person nearby, his name is...

Oliver! Alive!
He looks like an olive,

But when he gives
Me a high five,
I am back into a dream!
There is cotton candy,
But then I see a bee,
It looks like me.

But when I touch it,
It turns into a portal,
When I go in, I turn into a mortal.

Kian Lo (9)
Gunter Primary School, Pype Hayes

The Rainforest

T he stars glisten every night.
H ow can I stay inside?
E ven though it's not cold, I'm always told.

R ight, I should stay inside, but I see Suki.
A lthough it's dangerous, I'm still eager.
I n the rainforest, I see the dragon fly.
N ever going too high.
F rom the bottom of my heart, I will never go.
O n the clean river, the water will flow.
R ainy all night, I look down from a height.
E ven though I'm getting wet, I don't want to go yet.
S ee the dragon flying, glowing in the dark air.
T he rain smells like fresh cotton candy.

Chloe Hodgetts (8)
Gunter Primary School, Pype Hayes

Meeting Billie Eilish

My dream is to meet Billie Eilish,
Because she sings like birds,
Her hair is as black as ash,
Her voice is as sweet as candyfloss,
The crowd looks like it's dancing and prancing,
Whoop! And it sounds like the crowd is playing songs because the crowd is singing along,
Billie Eilish goes on and on, it goes non-stop but will come to an end,
The cheering gets louder as it gets to an end,
Soon the concert has finished,
And I am asked if I want to meet Billie Eilish, so I say yes,
I say the words: "You sing like birds and your voice is as sweet as cotton candy,"
And then we make friends, so she performs one of her unreleased songs.

Ollie Davis (8)
Gunter Primary School, Pype Hayes

The Constellations

C ould the sky be any brighter?
O n my own, the sky gets lighter.
N ever has the sky been like this.
S hining stars, I'll be sure not to miss.
T his is strange.
E xtraordinary, the stars are moving - what a change.
L earn that the stars don't move at all.
L earn that the stars are moving and they just might fall.
A fter a while, time moves fast.
T ime is moving, maybe for the last.
I n one minute, I slowly wake up.
O n my own in bed, what luck.
N ow I think, *what a dream*.
S o now I look at the sky where I've been.

Isha Adams (9)
Gunter Primary School, Pype Hayes

My Dream To Go To WrestleMania And The Championship

I'm standing in a big ring, and all I hear is chants, and the bell goes! *Ding! Ding! Ding!* Then I look ahead of me and see Cody Rhodes.

Then he comes up to me and hits a punch and a kick, but I hit my signature - a spear. Then I hit him with a punch, bang him, and go up to the white top rope and frog splash him.

Then I cover him for one, two, and three and jump in victory with my family and say, "I am the new champion." And everybody acknowledges me.

One day, I - The Machine - am standing in the middle of the ring with a microphone, and I say, "I have a cousin joining me to win tag team championships, so now call us undefeatable!"

Aadham Daud (8)
Gunter Primary School, Pype Hayes

Is To Be Everything

I want to be everything in the world, even the king! The sun is dancing in the sky. The waves clash as the tide comes out.
My house is made out of food for walls and smelly socks for mugs. It has strawberries for a door, it has pizza for a roof and it has chocs for sunglasses.
The stars twinkle in the night. People come in with a bang. The snow was waking and so was the sun. People slurped their drinks, rain dripped on someone's head. People help all day, every day when they need help.
The sun is as hot as Africa and the other hot countries of the world. The wavy waves are super soggy. The sand is as straight as a booklet. The snow is as cold as Antarctica.

T J Cox (8)
Gunter Primary School, Pype Hayes

Mesmet

In a beautiful magical land,
Where the creatures of Mesmet glance,
The unicorns and pegasus dance in the shimmering sky,
The mermaids swim in their sparkling pond and sing all day long.

The Glyphs and Alvis play in the snow, but are sent home when it gets cold,
The fairies go to their castle and invite Darity who comes over with friends for a party.

An evil shape-shifting wizard lizard called Jill comes,
He attacks the town to take the crown to be the king,
But a Glyph and her friends, Carbie, Sunshine, Sen, Loy, Kipper and Locki, save Mesmet,
Jill lost and was banished to the Lost Island.

Rhema Theophilus Okere (9)
Gunter Primary School, Pype Hayes

My Dream Is To Live By The Beach

My dream is to live by the beach
At night it's as cold as ice
The waves will float
Water will be as cold as ice
The sea goes whoosh
It is as hot as fire
The sea is as calm as it can be
The sky is as blue as sky
The waves go over the sand
The sun hangs in the sky like a peach
The waves go and dance at the edge of the sand
Looking pretty sky
Where the sun smiles in the sky
When every day I look at the beautiful view
Looking at the children laughing
When the sun shines in our eyes
I look at the sky shining blue as the sea
The sun shines in my eyes.

Hannah Khan (7)
Gunter Primary School, Pype Hayes

Dancing Pandas

Pandas are dancing as crazy as a clown,
If you want to be happy I suggest you stick around,
They're wearing pink tutus and baby pink pointe shoes,
While playing around when their teacher comes in,

"What are you doing?"
The pandas feel like a daisy being stomped on,
Their tutus went down and their teacher frowned,
As soon as they looked at each other, they laughed and laughed,
Their teacher said, "I quit,"
But that's not the end,
With a bang, a boom and a whoosh with a push,
We will be back with a big boosh.

Juliet Jenkinson (9)
Gunter Primary School, Pype Hayes

Pink Flying Unicorns In Candyland

Unicorns fly high
Mostly some of them fly then say bye
Candy, candy ever so sweet
Candyland is just a treat
Unicorns doing jumping jacks
Unicorns eat candyfloss, that's a fact.

Play with the unicorns with my friend
I hope this day will never end
Otherwise, it will be a tragic end
Build a candy house, chop, chop, chop
Oh no, quick, get a mop
I want to flop because nobody's got a mop.

It's lunchtime, get a sweet sugary treat
I know it's not good for my teeth but it's good for me!

Chloe Evans (9)
Gunter Primary School, Pype Hayes

Fairy Mystery

F ar away in a magic land,
A little pink and purple light flashing bright,
I get a bit scared,
R ustling sigh and a sad sob,
Y ou finally see it is a fairy.

M ini magic here and there,
Y ou see a spark of dust glistening in the city,
S uper trees all around glistening in the dark,
T ime for tea and you get a sweet treat,
E xtravagant unicorn pink and white,
R eally this is a fairy and a unicorn,
Y ou should come along to meet them too.

Erin Clarke (9)
Gunter Primary School, Pype Hayes

Hawaiian Beaches

My dream is to live in Hawaii and see the Hawaiian trees and the sandy beach with the greenish-blue ocean
Kids playing from far away, they look in slow-motion
The sun shines like stars in the sky
Coconuts being drunk, coconut meat being eaten
The waves rushing along the shore like children playing
Beachballs being kicked in the air like the sunset rising from the sky
The beach is as calm as can be, seeing waves rise from the sea
People buying cold drinks and eating ice cream by the beach
As the sun shines like a giant peach.

Savannah Grant (8)
Gunter Primary School, Pype Hayes

I Am Trapped In A Nightmare

I will be trapped in a nightmare.
I will never get out of this.
Bang! Smash! Boo hoo!
A nightmare of dreams I will never get out of.
Oh, it's just a dream.
Or is it?
I'm just going on a walk.
Yipee! Yes!
Just keep walking.
Oh no! Ahh!
There is a dead body.
I better run now.
Wait! Is that Reggie Smejy Eggy, my best lad?
Why you look so numb, bro?
So, um, yeah, so, basically,
I was making dinner and the pan exploded with the house too.
So, yes you can stay at mine.

Aurora Maxfield-Foster (9)
Gunter Primary School, Pype Hayes

My Dream

My dream is to live in a world of animals,
The animals are cute and fluffy,
In my world it's bright and sunny, all the bears do is eat lots of honey,
In this world of happy animals, there is a soft sandy beach, the sea is as blue as the beautiful sky,
All the animals play in the soft sand and the beautiful blue water,
There are dogs, cats, rabbits, tigers, lions, hamsters,
And any other animals you can think of,
The sun dances in the blue sky.

I'miah-Milan Jackson Griffiths (8)
Gunter Primary School, Pype Hayes

The Land Of Candy

My dream is to live in a candy land,
And the sand is as soft as cotton candy,
The sea is as loud as a lion's roar and as the sea collides,
The sea goes push, and the sun is as bright as can be,
Me and my friends Aria, Imiah and Rome have so much fun,
When I am there, the water splashes so much,
Me and my friends get so wet,
We need to leave,
Me and my friends get so sad,
But we have to say goodbye.

Cheyenne Davies (8)
Gunter Primary School, Pype Hayes

My Scary Dream

Where am I?
Wow, this is cool but why are they in the sky jumping and hopping?
But wait, they come, turning around, aaargh!
They're scary athletes now
They are chasing me everywhere, they won't stop at all
Someone help me, please
They grin and bite me
I'm hurt, I have a mark on my arm
It is bleeding very badly
Then wait, I am awake
Wait, it's a dream
Phew, it's a dream.

Aleeza Minhas (9)
Gunter Primary School, Pype Hayes

My Dream Is To Live By A Beautiful Beach

Where the sun hung in the sky like a giant peach,
I saw wobbly waves floating people as if in the air,
The girl's green, fresh pear tangled in her brown hair,
Her brown hair flew into her mouth as she ate the pear,
When I saw the wave whoosh on the sand, I felt a scare,
The air smelled nice,
Sadly, the girl had lice,
Her shirt came at a high price,
The boys stood frozen like ice.

Amelia Reynolds (8)
Gunter Primary School, Pype Hayes

Chickensaur

Chickensaur is strong like a gorilla
And smells like fried chicken
It sings to its eggs
Any animal would try to beg
Snap, crash, wild animals get
In its jaw like a pro
In a cave where people go
It would write letters to go
Getting free meals over time
A police officer said, "This is a crime,"
Running as fast as a bolt
Hunting like a shark.

Sebastian Ullah (9)
Gunter Primary School, Pype Hayes

The Fast Tortoise

I am a tortoise as fast as a hare
Quick, don't be late, please don't have a scare
I'm a hare and my friend is a bear
And he has lots of hair
Please don't make a scare of the grizzly bear
Otherwise, you will be eaten by the bear
And if he does then say goodbye to Mr Hare
But now he's inside the grizzly bear
Eating a big, ripe pear.

Bobby Thomas (9)
Gunter Primary School, Pype Hayes

Astronauts And Pirates

Enter the scary world of pirates and astronauts, stuck and shocked in the desert.
They say, "What's happened to space?"
They reply, "Nowhere, no people, just sand and me."
Then I see a pirate, and he says, "Follow me, I can show you the way to the beach."
We finally arrive, then I hear some *bangs* and then a *crash*.

Zayn Shaikh (8)
Gunter Primary School, Pype Hayes

Footballer

My dream is to be a footballer.
Where the stadium is full of fans,
The footballers run on the field.
When the defender is the shield,
The strikers can not shoot.
The field is as green as the grass,
The fans roaring to cheer the players on.
Scoring a goal for my team,
At the stadium by the stream,
Is as good as gold can be.

Lucas Ma (8)
Gunter Primary School, Pype Hayes

My Dream

As the butterfly flutters around me,
Birds tweeting in the trees,
Sidelia, my best friend, smiles as the sun glows with joy.
Horses, ponies and unicorns galloping in herds,
Sparkling and glowing, around this magical world full of joy.
As we smile at the sparkling gold stars,
Shooting stars glide through the sky,
As we sleep under the sky.

Aisha Adetona (8)
Gunter Primary School, Pype Hayes

A Miracle

A beach is dancing on the sand
A queen is bathing on the land
A king in shallow sand
A princess cooking with a pan
A prince is watching, drooling over the food
They all see a shadow so they go home.
Everybody was waiting for them
Everybody was so happy, they all lived happily by the beach
They were so happy they went to sleep.

Kalelsi Macalum Francis (8)
Gunter Primary School, Pype Hayes

Selling Ice Cream In A Van

Selling ice cream in the hot weather
Watch them eat ice cream
Making whippy ice cream with a flake, even strawberry sauce
Giving out slushies in different flavours
Giving Oreo ice cream and it's delicious
I come at 4pm or 5:58pm
I make sure to come out with money to buy some
Make sure to listen for the sound.

Zac Moore (8)
Gunter Primary School, Pype Hayes

Flying Unicorn At School

It was like any normal day at school,
But all of a sudden,
It felt more magical,
Is it a flying bird?
Is it a planet?
No, it's a flying unicorn!

One day at school,
I saw a beautiful unicorn,
With rainbow hair,
But it was up in the sky flying,
When I came back, it was gone!

Kirsten Dhliwayo (9)
Gunter Primary School, Pype Hayes

Living By The Beach

My dream is to live by the beach and be an engineer and make new creations and be famous.
I want everyone to be happy, and I also want the sea to be sparkling and bright blue, and I want the sun to be bright as yellow.
And I also want the sea to be as clean as it can be and I also want to live in a caravan!

Ibrahim Hedjem (8)
Gunter Primary School, Pype Hayes

A Zoo Open Day: My Dream Is To Be A Zookeeper

I want to look after the giraffes
I feel happy and kind
The giraffes are smiling
The giraffes are running around
The people are stroking the tame animals
The animals are sitting in the sand
I feel proud about being a zookeeper.

Aria-Rae Delaney (7)
Gunter Primary School, Pype Hayes

The Very Sweet Sweety Land

My dream is to live in a big sweet sweety land,
And the grass is as soft as candyfloss,
And the clouds are made of fluffy bubblegum,
And we are having so much fun,
And we bought something and we are done.

Freya Jordan (8)
Gunter Primary School, Pype Hayes

Untitled

My dream is to live in a house on the beach.
I love to eat a peach when my dreams are of sweets.
I want to live by the beach so I can see the waves crash and flash.
I play in the sand and wave my hand.

Weronika Aiken (8)
Gunter Primary School, Pype Hayes

The Territory

In the territory, there lies a mythical animal
That has four legs
And that can eat you in a millisecond
And that can talk,
And it is a gorgon.

Michael Waltham (9)
Gunter Primary School, Pype Hayes

Untitled

Bounce! The ball goes in the hoop
We won, we are the champions
Now we have to win again
Aww, I fainted from all this hard work.

Rhyleigh-Marie Thompson (9)
Gunter Primary School, Pype Hayes

YoungWriters® Est. 1991

YOUNG WRITERS INFORMATION

We hope you have enjoyed reading this book – and that you will continue to in the coming years.

If you're a young writer who enjoys reading and creative writing, or the parent of an enthusiastic poet or story writer, do visit our website **www.youngwriters.co.uk**. Here you will find free competitions, workshops and games, as well as recommended reads, a poetry glossary and our blog.

If you would like to order further copies of this book, or any of our other titles, then please give us a call or visit **www.youngwriters.co.uk**.

Young Writers
Remus House
Coltsfoot Drive
Peterborough
PE2 9BF
(01733) 890066
info@youngwriters.co.uk

YoungWritersUK YoungWritersCW
youngwriterscw youngwriterscw